For Samuel – J.P.

Note from the compiler:
I love words and books and would read anything as a child.
I think words are magic and I hope the delight I experience
when I have a new idea for a poem or story will never leave me.

Copyright in this collection © Joan Poulson 2001
Illustrations copyright © Kelly Waldek 2001
Book copyright © Hodder Wayland 2001

Published in Great Britain in 2001
by Hodder Wayland, an imprint of
Hodder Children's Books
This edition published in 2002

The right of Joan Poulson to be identified as the
compiler and Kelly Waldek as the illustrator of this Work
has been asserted by them in accordance with the
Copyright, Designs and Patents Act 1988.

British Library Cataloguing in Publication Data
Sling a Jammy Doughnut
1. Children's poetry, English – Pictorial works
I. Poulson, Joan
821.9'14'08

ISBN: 0 7502 3260 9

Printed by Wing King Tong, Hong Kong.

Hodder Children's Books
A division of Hodder Headline Limited
338 Euston Road, London NW1 3BH

Sling a Jammy Doughnut

Compiled by Joan Poulson

Illustrated by Kelly Waldek

HODDER
Wayland

an imprint of Hodder Children's Books

Sling a Jammy Doughnut

(To the tune of: *Sing a Song of Sixpence*)

Sling a jammy doughnut
Up into the sky,
Splat into a jumbo jet
Learning how to fly;
When the cockpit opens
And the pilot checks his wings,
He says, "Don't throw the squashy ones,
I only like the rings!"

Dave Ward

Dinner on Space Day

Board your rocket. Take your place.
Today your dinner's from outer-space.

Sausage meteors in Yorkshire craters
With crispy asteroid potatoes.

Moondust gravy and Pluto peas
With a sprinkling of grated lunar cheese.

Shortbread aliens from Mars.
Chocolate cookies shaped like stars.

Fasten your seatbelts. Take your place.
Today your dinner's from outer-space.

John Foster

Choosing Food

What do you want to eat?
Would you like some meat?
Or maybe something sweet?
What do you want...
What do you want...
What do you want to eat?

We'll buy it
And fry it
And tuck in
And try it.

How do you feel
About that for a meal?

We'll make it
And bake it
And slice it
And take it.

How do you feel
About that for a meal?

We'll baste it
And taste it
'Cause we mustn't
Waste it.

So how do you feel...
How do you feel...
How do you feel
About that for a meal?

What do you want to eat?
Would you like some meat?
Or maybe something sweet?
What do you want...
What do you want...
What do you want to eat?

Nick Toczek

Fast Food

At the burger shop
they sell fast food –

Hot dogs sprint
the hundred metres
in ten seconds flat.
Fat chicken nuggets
set the pace
for Olympic races.
Hamburgers hurtle
over hurdles.
Burly baked potatoes
star in the decathlon,
flexing their muscles.
And no one dares tussle
with grilled sausages
that fare well
in the marathon.

Yes, the food is so fast
it's past your lips
before you can ask
for a bag of chips.

Pie Corbett

Nothing Beatsa Pizza!

Some go mad for fish and chips
Chicken nuggets, dripping dips
Others go for beans on toast
But there's one thing I love most
My advice, just grab a slice
Nothing beatsa pizza!

Pizza fat or pizza skinny
Pizza maxi, pizza mini
Eat it out or eat it in
Pizza all around your chin
Pizza gooey, pizza chewy
Nothing beatsa pizza!

Pizza bigger than your plate
Pizza shared with all your mates
Eat it cold or eat it hot
Pizza perfect, scoff the lot!
Pizza cheesy, goes down easy
Nothing beatsa pizza!

Paul Bright

The Greedy Giant

There lives this giant who
wears enormous eleven-league boots,
who strides across the mountain tops
sporting purple, pin-striped suits.

There lives this giant who
throws javelins for miles
Whose hair is like a hawthorn hedge,
who never smiles.

There lives this giant who
drinks rivers like ginger pop,
who sucks on stars like gold lollipops
and doesn't know when to stop.

There lives this giant who
likes dinosaurs for starters,
who spits out all the gnawed-on bones,
eats dragon cakes for afters.

There lives this giant who
has a voice as loud as thunder,
who storms and shouts and bellows with rage –
why so bad-tempered, I wonder?

The reason is – this giant's too fat,
saw a frock and went to buy it,
but though it's as wide as a circus tent,
to wear it, she'll have to diet!

Moira Andrew

Feeling Peckish

My greedy sister
turned into a hen.

She was looking in the biscuit tin
for cookies
when her fingers turned to feathers
and her arms to wings.

Now she lives in the garden
pecking cabbage stalks and things
that hens like to eat.

She claws the lawn for worms
with her scaly feet.

Irene Rawnsley

Daddy's Gone to Market

Daddy's gone to market,
Mummy's gone to sea,
Brother's eating sausages,
One, two, three.

Granny's in the kitchen
Making bread and tea,
There's a monkey in the shed
But he can't catch me.

Valerie Bloom

Anti-gravity Gravy

Anti-gravity gravy
is wonderful. It's new.
And yes, of course, it's just the sauce
to liven up a stew.

Anti-gravity gravy
will fill you with delight,
for, if you take it with your lunch
you'll end up feeling light.

Anti-gravity gravy
will keep your spirits up.
But when you're trying to stir it,
it won't stay in the cup.

It's fabulous, it's flavoursome,
it's groovy and it's great.
The only problem is it simply
won't stay on the plate.

It spirals slowly upwards
to float above the table,
so put some on your mashed potatoes
if you think you're able.

It rises and it hovers
and drifts about with ease.
You'll puzzle over how to pour it
neatly on your peas.

Anti-gravity gravy
may serve up a surprise
by gushing from the gravy-boat
and squirting in your eyes.

But, of it's quirky qualities,
the thing you'll find the worst,
is, if you want to try it,
you'll have to catch it first.

Tony Mitton

The Singing Sausage

"It's a grungy day," grumped Sausage.
"It's a grey-grungy day
and I'm just on my way
to sulk and snooze in a soft bread roll
because I haven't got a friend!
There's no one around for a clever
little Sausage to play with."

What about me?

"Was that a squeak?" said Sausage,
taking a peek
through a crack in the fence.

What about me?

On a tree... swinging...
red and round and all alone
among the peaches and plums:
one tiny tomato.

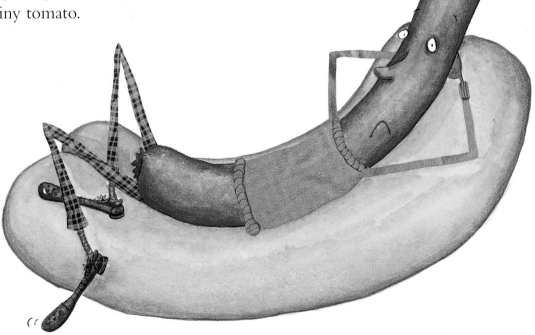

What about me?
It isn't very good, you know
to be alone
on a peachy-plum tree
when you're a tomato.

"Oh!" whispered Sausage.
And, "Oh!" he said again.
"Would you like a friend?"

Hey! Yippee! whistled Tomato
and wriggled and rolled... until *Plip!*
she tumbled to the ground.

"You are my friend!" Sausage said,
so happy he turned red and ssssizzzzled.

You're sssinging! laughed Tomato.

"I'm sssinging!" Sausage grinned.

Then away they rolled together,
ssssinging and *sizzzzling,*
giggling and jiggling...
We can sing! We can sing!

Joan Poulson

Seedy Story

Saucerful of mustard seed,
jam-jar full of beans;
all we'll have to eat next week
is greens, greens, GREENS!

Sprouting seeds inside the dish,
I know what this means!
Sprouts and shoots and leafy tops
and greens, greens, GREENS!

Judith Nicholls

The Dancing Carrot

The beetroot was getting married
The celery squealed with delight
The carrot stood up to dance a jig
And the horseradish whistled all night!

Traditional Czech translated by Andrew Fusek Peters

Plant Food

The Thing in the greenhouse
Eats *bonemeal*.
That's a meal that's made out of bone...
Its long green tendrils reach up to the sun
Its long roots lie under the stones.

The Thing in the greenhouse
Gets hungry.
Dad feeds and waters it each day.
But I'm not going into the greenhouse
In case I get in its way...

The Thing in the greenhouse gets bigger
And bigger and bigger, you see.
In my dreams I can hear it crunching the bones
Like a beast – and it's coming for me...

Jan Dean

Hog in a Wood

Big black hog in a wood
On a truffle hunt
Head stuck deep in the earth –
Grunt, snort, grunt.

Oh, a hog's in heaven when his tongue
Is wrapped around a truffle.
His tail uncurls and his hog heart
Performs a soft-shoe shuffle.

Big black hog in a wood
Chewing muddy truffles.
Great snout nosing them out –
Sniff, snuff, snuffles.

Adrian Mitchell

The Sweet

I've found a sweet
In my jeans' pocket
It could be a toffee
Or what's left
Of a sherbet rocket.

It's all covered
In fluff and other stuff
And stuck to some stones
I found in the street
But it's still a sweet.

Scrape off the fluff
And the slime
And all that stuff
Till it looks almost clean

And just
Pop it in.

Tony Bradman

Creative Cooking

A creative cook from Anguilla
in all his soups stirred sarsaparilla.
Pepper was his favourite spice.
He mixed it into puddings and rice
till it all tasted awful similla.

Debjani Chatterjee

No Eggs Today

If you come from Nigeria,
from the tribe of Yoruba,
you'll never have eggs at a meal

for there's an age-old belief
that a child who eats eggs will steal
and forever be known as THIEF!

Peggy Poole

The Mouse

The mouse that runs through the dust on the floor is dead.
I miss his footprints in my house, they were always there,
small spidery cuts in the thin fine dust
That floated through sunbeams from the rafters above.
Now his hole is empty and bare.
No one to eat my left-over crusts,
And the cat licks her lips in the chair.

Mike Harding

The Carnival's Come

The Carnival's come!
The Carnival's come!
Stamp your feet
And bang your drum,
Join the queues
For party food –

Chicken baked
And fried and stewed,
Buttered corn
    And salted chips,
    Spicy soup
    On burning lips,
      Roasted peppers,
      Juicy dates,
        Melon smiles
        On paper plates,
        Golden fruits
          From sunshine lands,
          Candyfloss
          In sticky hands,
            Sugared stacks
            Of doughnut rings
              Sweet enough
              For queens and kings,
              Smoky smells
                From barbecues,

Sniff the air
And join the queues,
Stamp your feet
And bang your drum,
The Carnival's come!
The Carnival's come!

Clare Bevan

Guy Forks

The hill above London town
Is filled with a feast of light,
Catherine Wheels are Wagon Wheels
Spinning like sweets in the night.

Sparklers dance their sherbet fizz,
Blown out by the wind so sour,
Rockets leap like liquorice lace
And explode in a sugar shower.

Bangers go Plop! in a mushy mash,
The flames are eating the Guy,
Chestnuts tap-dance on the coals,
And taste like heaven! I sigh.

Hot dogs warm as the bonfire,
With mustard sharp as the cold,
November the Fifth is a banquet
For this hungry seven-year-old.

Andrew Fusek Peters

Moon Cakes for Trung Thu

(You say *Troong Too* – it means Moon Festival)

In Vietnam, the moon glowing white
fills the children with great delight.
For an autumn full moon, big and bright,
brings cakes and sweets. *It's Trung Thu Night*.

Drums and cymbals and dancing feet,
star-shaped lanterns lighting the street.
Stalls sell Moon Cakes for us to eat –
fish and flower shapes, sticky and sweet.

Wearing masks, no one knows who is who:
"Who's there?" "It's me!" "Who are you?"
A sky full of stars, full moon shining through:
Hunter's Moon, Harvest Moon, bright Trung Thu.

Mandy Coe

I Didn't Want to Come to Your Party, Anyway!

May your jelly never wobble
May your custard turn to lumps
May your toffee go all gooey
And your mousse come out in bumps.

May your pancakes hit the ceiling
May your cocoa crack the cup
May your lollies turn to water
And your sponge cake soak it up.

May the icing on your birthday cake
Set hard as Superglue
And they'll tell me, *Wish we hadn't
Been invited – just like you!*

Rita Ray

Manners

Don't eat custard with your fingers
When invited out to tea.
It isn't right, it's not polite.
Eat your fingers separately!

Kaye Umansky

Universal Instant Gloop™

Universal Instant Gloop™
tomorrow's food today
makes anything you fancy
the new convenient way!

No mess, no wait, no waste!
No need to scrape or peel!
Stir in a flavour cube to taste –
it makes any meal!

Butter, jam and toast;
burger, sauce and bun;
one pack of Gloop™ makes everything –
so simple, fast and fun!

Universal Instant Gloop™
sets your taste buds free!
Why not try blue curried jelly
or square purple peas!

Amaze your friends, delight yourself,
with one wonder packet on your shelf!
All you need is a handy scoop
of Universal Instant Gloop.™

Dave Calder

Gloop™

INGREDIENTS

Joan Poulson and Hodder Wayland would like to thank
the following for contributing to this collection:

Sling a Jammy Doughnut © Dave Ward 2001
Dinner on Space Day © John Foster 2001
Choosing Food © Nick Toczek 2001
Fast Food © Pie Corbett 2001
Nothing Beatsa Pizza © Paul Bright 2001
The Greedy Giant © Moira Andrew 2001
Feeling Peckish © Irene Rawnsley 2001
Daddy's Gone to Market © Valerie Bloom 2001
Anti-gravity Gravy © Tony Mitton 2001
The Singing Sausage © Joan Poulson 2001
Seedy Story © Judith Nicholls 2000
The Dancing Carrot © Andrew Fusek Peters 2001
Plant Food © Jan Dean 2001
Hog in a Wood © Adrian Mitchell. Available in *Balloon Lagoon and the Magic Islands of Poetry* (Orchard Books, 1997). Reprinted by permission of PFD on behalf of Adrian Mitchell. Educational Health Warning! Adrian Mitchell asks that none of his poems are used in connection with any examinations whatsoever.
The Sweet © Tony Bradman, 1989. First published in *All Together Now!* (Penguin, 1989). Reproduced by permission of The Agency (London) Ltd.
Creative Cooking © Debjani Chatterjee 2001
No Eggs Today © Peggy Poole 2001
The Mouse © Mike Harding 2001
The Carnival's Come © Clare Bevan 2001
Guy Forks © Andrew Fusek Peters 2001
Moon Cakes for Trung Thu © Mandy Coe 2001
I Didn't Want to Come to Your Party, Anyway © Rita Ray 2001
Manners © Kaye Umansky 2001
Universal Instant Gloop™ © Dave Calder 2001